T0078877

Carol Arrangements for Choir and Orchestra

by Joseph M. Martin, Mark Hayes and Pepper Choplin

Orchestrations by Brant Adams, Mark Hayes and Stan Pethel

Exclusively Distributed By

7777 W. Bluemound Rd. P.O. Box 13819 Milwaukee, WI 53213

Copyright © 2014 by HAL LEONARD-MILWIN MUSIC CORP. & HAL LEONARD CORPORATION
All Rights Reserved. International Copyright Secured.

Visit Shawnee Press Online at
www.shawneepress.com

FOREWORD

Christmas wraps its arms of song around us with loving embrace each year just as the cold of winter begins to chill our spirits. December's familiar carols and seasonal songs encircle us with the warmth of memories and bring promise to our spiritual quests. The treasured rituals of Advent and Christmas are always best when adorned with music and shared with others. In the lighting of candles, the sharing of Scripture and the singing of our songbook of faith, we affirm our purposes as people of promise and praise.

This gathering of carols for choir can be a useful resource for your concert planning. Whether used for sacred services or in concert hall settings, we trust that the variety reflected in these selections will bring delight to your events. All selections are fully orchestrated bringing a festive performance option for holiday gatherings. From reflective cradle carols to joyful acclamations of worship, these well-known songs of the season will be treasured repertoire for years to come.

Let Christmas Begin!

Joseph M. Martin

JOY TO THE WORLD

for S.A.T.B. voices, accompanied

Tune: **ANTIOCH**
by GEORGE F. HANDEL (1685-1759)
Arranged by
JOSEPH M. MARTIN (BMI)

Words by
ISAAC WATTS (1674-1748), *alt.*

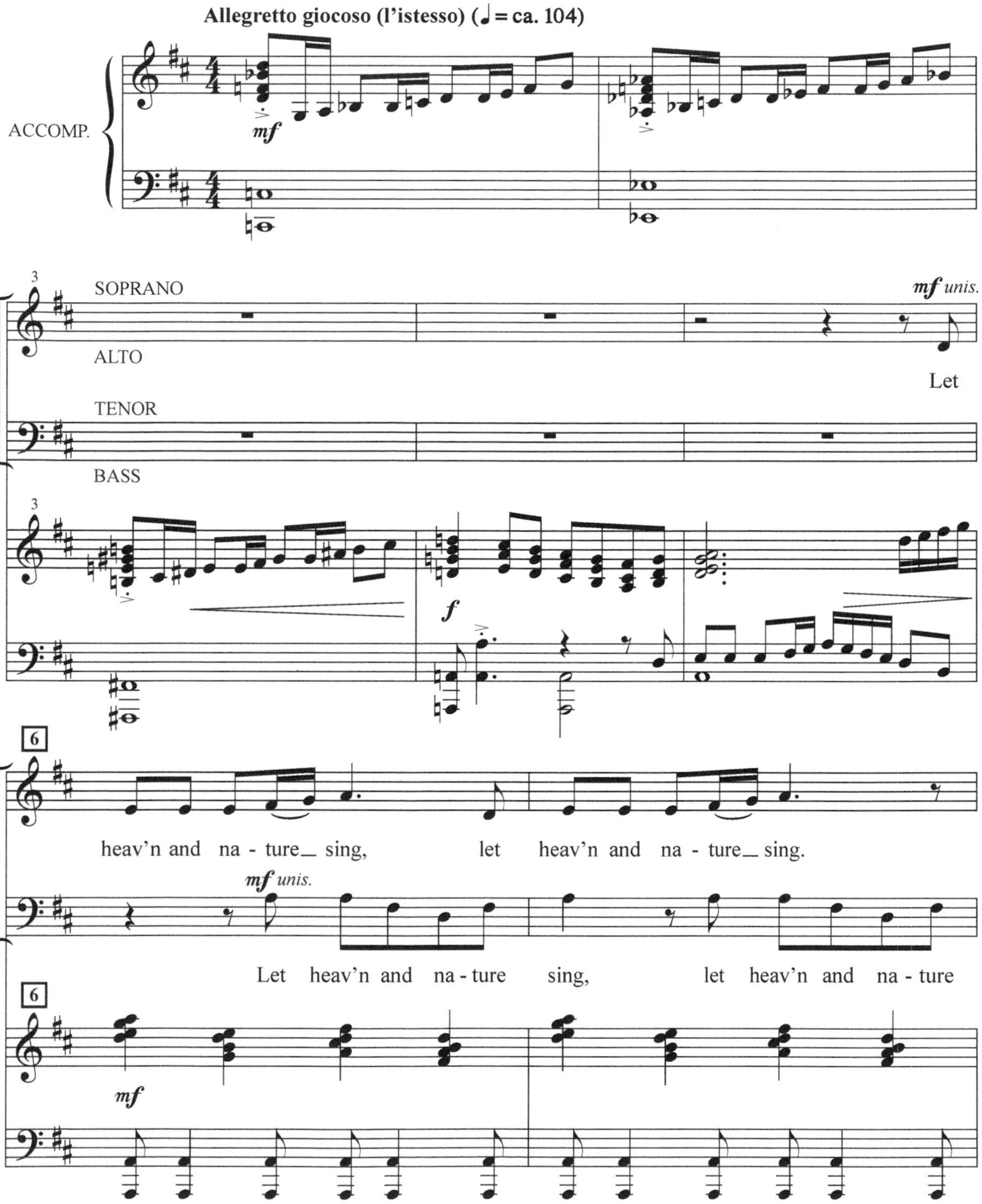

3

SOPRANO

ALTO

mf unis.

Let

TENOR

BASS

3

f

6

heav'n and na - ture_ sing, let heav'n and na - ture_ sing.

mf unis.

Let heav'n and na - ture sing, let heav'n and na - ture

6

mf

Copyright © 2002, 2007 by Malcolm Music
(A Division of Shawnee Press, Inc.)
All Rights Reserved. International Copyright Secured.

Duplication of this publication is illegal, and duplication is not granted by the CCLI, LicenSing or OneLicense.net license.

8
cresc.
Let ev-'ry na-tion, all cre - a - tion, sing for joy!
cresc.
sing. Ev-'ry na-tion, all cre - a - tion, sing for joy!
8
cresc.
11
f
Joy to the world, the Lord is come! Let earth re - ceive her
f
11
f
14
mf
King. Let ev - 'ry heart pre -
mf
Sing for joy!
14
mf

16
pare Him room, and heav'n and na - ture sing, and
Sing for joy! Sing un - to the Lord. Let heav'n and na - ture
16
18
heav'n and na - ture sing, and heav'n, and heav'n and
f
sing, let heav'n and na - ture, heav'n, and heav'n and
18
f
20
na - ture sing.
na - ture sing.
20

23
legato
mf unis.
Joy to the earth, the Sav - ior reigns!
mf unis.
Joy to the earth, the Sav - ior reigns! Let
23
mf
25
f
poco rit.
mp
Let all their songs, their songs em - ploy while
f
all their songs em - ploy.
25
f
poco rit.
27
a tempo
fields and floods, rocks, hills, and plains re -
mp
unis.
Al - le - lu - ia!
27
a tempo
mp

unis. cresc. poco a poco
peat the sound-ing joy, re - peat the sound-ing joy re - peat the sound-ing
cresc. poco a poco
cresc. poco a poco
joy!
with great celebration
unis.
Joy to the world! Joy to the world!
unis.
Joy to the world! Joy to the
with great celebration

*Original is "He"

mf unis.
makes the na - tions prove the
mf unis.
glo - ries of
mp
and
His right - eous - ness,
sub. mf
won - ders of His love, and won - ders of His love, and
The won - ders,
mf
The won - ders
mp

48
f
won - ders, won - ders of His
won - ders, the won - ders of His
f
won - ders, won - ders of His
48
f
50
love.
love.
love.
50
cresc.
53
ff
Joy to the world! Joy to the world!
ff
53
ff

55
Joy to the world for Christ the
57
Lord is born! Joy to the world! Joy to the
59
world!
fff

commissioned to the glory of God in honor of Rev. G. Alan Benson, celebrating his retirement on June 16, 2004 after 14 years of dedicated service as Minister of Music, First United Methodist Church of Griffin, Georgia, with deep appreciation by the friends of the FUMC music community

LET ALL MORTAL FLESH KEEP SILENCE

for S.A.T.B. voices, female solo, accompanied

Words from the Liturgy of St. James, 5th century
Translation by
Gerard Moultrie (1829-1885), *alt.*

Tune: **PICARDY**
Traditional French Carol
Arranged by
JOSEPH M. MARTIN (BMI)

Copyright © 2004, 2008 by Malcolm Music
(A Division of Shawnee Press, Inc.)
International Copyright Secured. All Rights Reserved.

Duplication of this publication is illegal, and duplication is not granted by the CCLI, LicenSing or OneLicense.net licenses.

15
for with bless-ing in His___ hand
Christ our God to earth de-
18
(end solo)
scend - ing,
our full hom-age to de - mand.
pp
21
Slowly, with sadness (♩= ca. 69)
p
mp
25

28
SOPRANO and ALTO
p unis.
King of kings, yet born of Ma - ry, as of old on earth He
TENOR and BASS
28
p
r.h.
31
stood.
(p)
Lord of lords and King of kings,
mp unis.
Lord of lords, in hu - man ves - ture,
31
mp
34
mf cresc.
in the bod - y and the blood.
mf cresc.
34
mf cresc.

*Original is "He"

45
mp
as the Light de - scend - eth
mp
as the Light of light de - scend - eth
45
47
cresc.
from the realms of end - less day
rit.
49
a tempo
mf
that the pow'rs of hell may
cresc.
mf
47
49
a tempo
cresc.
rit.
mf
50
van - ish as the shad - ows clear a - way,
unis.
unis.
50

53
f
as the shad - ows clear a - way.
56
57
59
ff
At His feet the six-winged_ ser - aph, cher - u - bim with watch - ful _

62
eye, veil their fac - es to the Pres - ence,
62
3
3
3
65
as with end-less voice they cry,
67
"Al - le - lu - ia! Al - le -
65
67
3
r.h.
68
lu - ia! Al - le - lu - ia!
Al - le - lu - ia, Lord Most
68
3
3

70
rit.
High!
Al - le - lu - ia, Lord Most High!
70
rit.
73
Slowly, with great power
ff
Al - le - lu - ia, Lord Most
ff
73
Slowly, with great power
ff
75
rit.
fff
High!
Al - le - lu - ia!"
fff
75
rit.
fff

BRING A TORCH, JEANETTE, ISABELLA

for S.A.T.B. voices, accompanied

Words:
Traditional French Carol, alt.

Tune:
UN FLAMBEAU JEANETTE, ISABELLA
Traditional French Melody
Arranged by
PEPPER CHOPLIN (ASCAP)

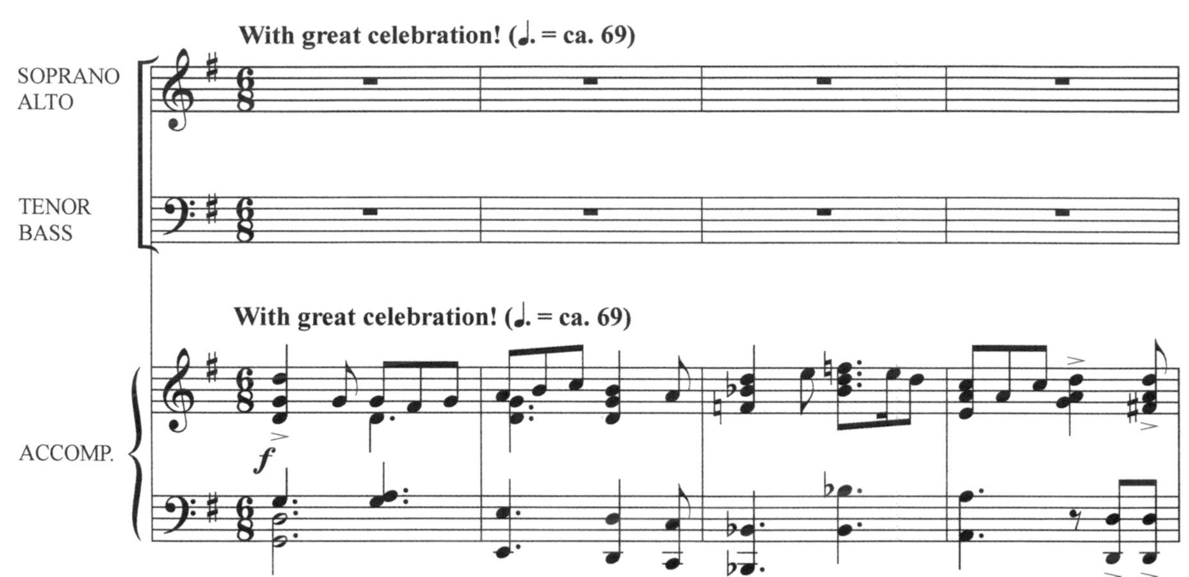

Copyright © 2014 by HAL LEONARD CORPORATION
International Copyright Secured All Rights Reserved

Duplication of this publication is illegal, and duplication is not granted by the CCLI, LicenSing or OneLicense.net licenses.

8
swift - ly and run. Christ is born, tell the folk of the vil - lage,
8
11
13
mf
Je - sus is born and Mar - y's call - ing: Ah! Ah!
mf
11
13
mf
14
Beau - ti - ful is the mo - ther! Ah! Ah! Beau - ti - ful is her
14

19
mf unis.
Child!
Has - ten now good folk of the vil - lage,
mf
mf unis.
You will find Him a -
has - ten now the Child to see.
27
sleep in the man - ger, qui - et - ly come and whis - per soft - ly. Hush, hush,

28
peace-ful - ly now He slum - bers. Hush, hush, peace-ful - ly now He
28
31
rit.
sleeps.
31
rit.
35
Smoothly (♩. = ca. 58)
mp unis.
Soft - ly now come un - to the sta - ble.
mp unis.
Soft - ly for a
35
Smoothly (♩. = ca. 58)
mp

39
41
mf
Look and see the beau-ty of hea - ven
mo - ment come.
43
mp
shin - ing in the face of Je - sus. Come, come,
46
accel.
wor-ship the ho - ly Sa - vior. Come, come, wor-ship the new - born

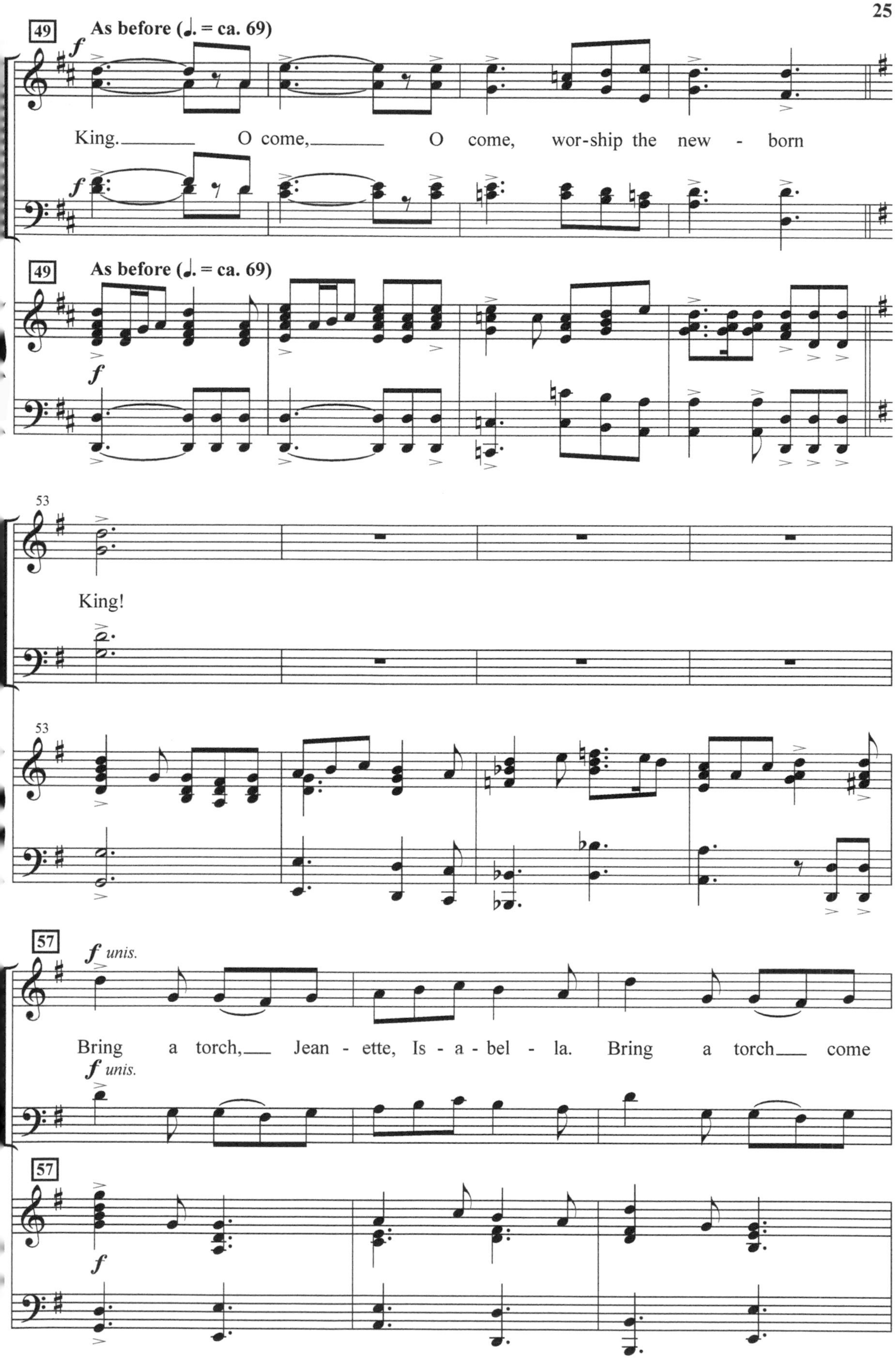
49
As before (♩. = ca. 69)
f
King. O come, O come, wor-ship the new - born
f
49
As before (♩. = ca. 69)
f
53
King!
53
57
f unis.
Bring a torch, Jean - ette, Is - a - bel - la. Bring a torch come
f unis.
57
f

60
swift - ly and run. From the throne of heav - en's glo - ry,
60
63
65
Christ came down that we may rise. So come, come,
63
65
66
join the ho - ly cho - rus. Come, come, join the heav - en
66

69
71
song.
Hal - le - lu - jah!
Hal - le - lu - jah!
Hal - le -
73
ff
Hal - le - lu - jah!
Hal - le - lu - jah,
hal - le - lu - jah,
hal - le -
lu - jah!
76
lu - jah,
hal - le - lu - jah!

HOW FAR IS IT TO BETHLEHEM?

for S.A.T.B. voices, accompanied

Words by
St. 1-2: FRANCES CHESTERTON (1875-1938), alt.
St. 3: CHRISTINA ROSSETTI (1830-1894)

Tune: STOWEY
Traditional English Melody
Arranged by
JOSEPH M. MARTIN (BMI)

Copyright © 2014 by HAL LEONARD - MILWIN MUSIC CORP.
International Copyright Secured. All Rights Reserved.

Duplication of this publication is illegal, and duplication is not granted by the CCLI, LicenSing or OneLicense.net licenses.

16
Is He with - in? If we lift the wood - en latch,
20
may we go in?
24
25
mp
Oo
TENOR
BASS
mp unis.
May we stroke the crea - tures there, ox - en, or
24
25

28
unis.
we watch like them and see Je - sus a -
sheep? May we watch like them and see Je - sus a -
28
32
poco rit.
p
34 Freely
sleep? If we touch His ti - ny hand,
p
sleep?
32
34 Freely
poco rit.
(Accompanist may double voices if desired.)
36
will He a - wake? Will He know we've come so far just for His
36

41
Tempo I
rit.
mf unis.
sake?
O
mf unis.
41
Tempo I
mp
rit.
45
With expressive sweep (♩ = ca. 84)
what can I give to Him, poor as I
45
With expressive sweep (♩ = ca. 84)
mf
48
am? If I were a shep - herd,
48

51
53
f
I'd bring a lamb. If I were a
wise man, I'd do my part. Yet
mf
54
57
what can I give to Him? Give Him my heart.

61
rit.
mp unis.
63 Slowly
Yet what can I give Him?
mp unis.
Yet what can I
61
63 Slowly
rit.
mp
66
p
Yet what can I give Him? I'll
give Him?
66
p
give Him my heart.
70
rit.
pp
I'll give Him my heart.
pp
70
pp
rit.

MASTERS IN THIS HALL

for S.A.T.B. voices, accompanied

Words by
WILLIAM MORRIS (1834-1896)

Traditional French Carol
Arranged by
MARK HAYES (ASCAP)

Copyright © 2003 by Harold Flammer Music
(A Division of Shawnee Press, Inc.)
International Copyright Secured All Rights Reserved

Duplication of this publication is illegal, and duplication is not granted by the CCLI, LicenSing or OneLicense.net licenses.

10
hear ye news to - day
brought from o - ver sea,
and
10
12
mp
ev - er I you pray:
Now - ell! Now - ell! Now - ell!
mp
12
mp
14
Now - ell sing we clear!
Hol - pen are all folk on earth,
born
14

16
is God's Son so dear.
16
mf
sub. p
18
18
mp
21
mp unis.
Go - ing o'er the hills,
through the milk - white snow,
mp unis.
Go - ing o'er the hills,
through the milk - white
21
mf
mp

23
heard I ewes bleat while the wind did blow.
snow, heard I ewes bleat while the wind did
23
25
mf
unis.
Now - ell! Now - ell! Now - ell! Now - ell sing we clear! Hol - pen
mf
blow. Now - ell! Now - ell! Now - ell! Now - ell sing we
25
mf
27
are all folk on earth, born is God's Son so dear.
unis.
clear! Hol - pen are all folk on earth, born is God's Son so
27

29
dear.
29
legato
31
33
mp
35
mf sing 1st time only
Shep - herds man - y an one
sing 2nd time only
mf
Quoth I, "Fel - lows mine,
35
mf

37
sat a - mong the sheep.
why this guise sit ye,
37
39
No man spake more word than
mak - ing but dull cheer,
39
41
they had been a - sleep.
shep - herds though ye be?"
41

43
S.
f
Now - ell! Now - ell!
A. f
Now - ell! Now - ell! Now - ell! Now - ell sing we
T.
f
Now - ell! Now - ell!
B. f
Now - ell! Now - ell! Now - ell! Now - ell sing we
43
f
46
Hol - pen are all folk on earth, born
clear! Hol - pen are all folk on earth, born
Hol - pen are all folk on earth, born
clear! Hol - pen are all folk on earth, born
46

49
ff
is God's Son so dear.
is God's Son so dear.
is God's Son so dear.
is God's Son so dear.
49
ff
51
mf playfully
54
SOPRANO
ALTO
TENOR
BASS
55
mf unis.
Shep - herds should of right
54
55
mp

56
leap and dance and sing. Thus to see ye sit
56
58
is a right strange thing. Quoth these fel - lows then, "To
mp unis.
Oo
58
60
Beth - l'em town we go to see a might - y Lord
60

62
63
lie in man - ger low."
mf
There - in did we see a
mf
64
sweet and good - ly may and a fair old man, up -
66
mp
Ah
on the straw she lay, and a lit - tle child

68
Ah
on her arm had she. "Wot ye who this is?"
68
70
71
mf
Now - ell! Now - ell! Now - ell!
said the hinds to me.
70
71
mf
72
Now - ell sing we clear! Hol - pen are all folk on earth, born
72

74
is God's Son so dear.
76
79
f unis.
This is Christ, the Lord, masters, be ye glad!
This is Christ, the Lord, masters, be ye glad!
79

81
Christ - mas is come in, and no folk should be sad.
81
83
Now - ell! Now - ell! Now - ell! Now - ell! Hol - pen
unis.
Now - ell! Now - ell! Now - ell! Now - ell sing we clear!
83
85
are all folk on earth, born is God's Son so dear.
85

87

ff

Now - ell! Now - ell! Now - ell! Now - ell sing we loud! God to -

ff

87

ff

89

ff

day hath poor folk raised and cast a -

ff

89

ff

91

fff

down the proud!

fff

91

fff

dedicated to my mother-in-law, Cleva Collar, and her family
in celebration of the life of Robert Jay Collar, who loved to sing

O HOLY NIGHT

for S.A.T.B. voices, accompanied

Tune: **CANTIQUE NOËL**
by ALDOLPHE ADAM (1803-1856)
Arranged by
JOSEPH M. MARTIN (BMI)

Words by
JOHN S. DWIGHT (1813-1893)

With freedom (𝅗𝅥 = ca. 54)

ACCOMP.

pp

6

rit.

11 **Peacefully (♩. = ca. 66)**

p

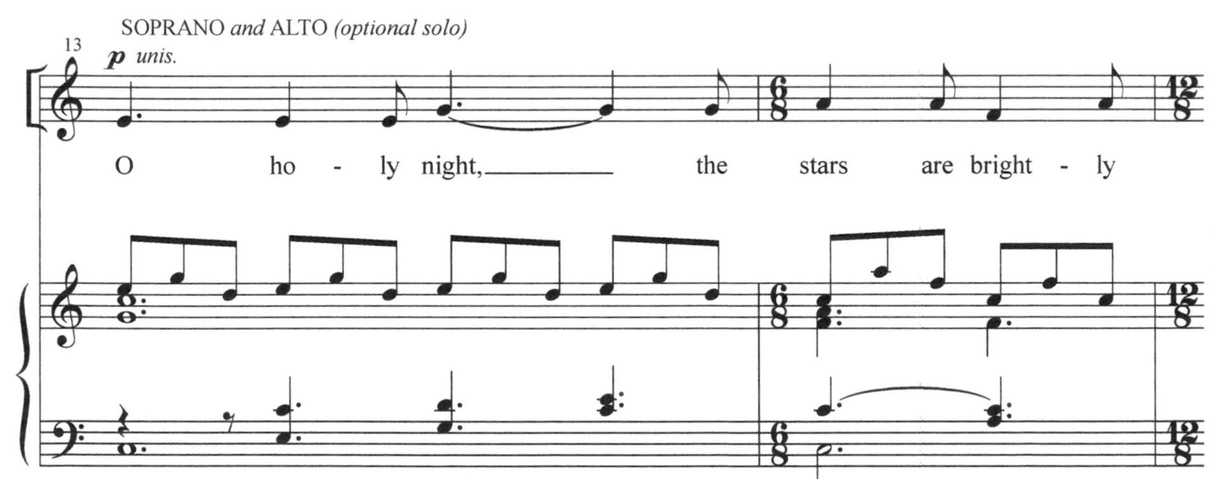

Copyright © 2007 by Malcolm Music
(A Division of Shawnee Press, Inc.)
All Rights Reserved. International Copyright Secured.

Duplication of this publication is illegal, and duplication is not granted by the CCLI, LicenSing or OneLicense.net license.

15
shin - ing. It is the night of the dear Sav - ior's
17
18
birth. Long lay the world in
19
sin and er - ror pin - ing, till He ap -
21
mp
peared and the soul felt its worth. A

23
thrill of hope, the wea - ry world re - joic - es, for
mp

(end solo)
25
yon - der breaks a new and glo - rious morn.

27
S.
A.
f
Fall on your knees. O
T.
B.
f
27
f

29
hear the an - gel voic - es. O
31
night di - vine, O
33
mf cresc. poco a poco
night when Christ was born. O
when Christ was, Christ was born.

35
rit.
ff
night di - vine, O
ff
35
ff
rit.
37
39 a tempo
f
mp
night, O night di - vine.
f
mp
37
39 a tempo
f
mp
40
p
Tru - ly He taught us to
p
40
p

42
love one an - oth - er. His law is
44
love and His gos - pel is peace.
46
God is our friend, for Christ is now our

48
mf
broth - er, and in His name all op-pres - sion shall
mf
48
mf
50
mp unis.
cresc. poco a poco
cease. Sweet hymns of joy in
mp unis.
cresc. poco a poco
50
mp
cresc. poco a poco
52
grate - ful cho - rus raise we. Let all with - in us
52

54 55

praise His ho - ly name. Christ is the

56

Lord! O praise His name for -

58

ev - er. O night di -

60
vine, O night when Christ was
when Christ was,
60
62
mf cresc. poco a poco
63
born. O night di -
mf cresc. poco a poco
Christ was born.
62
63
mf cresc. poco a poco
molto rit.
64
ff
vine, O night,
ff
64
ff
molto rit.

66
a tempo
mf
O night di - vine! O ho - ly
68
cresc. poco a poco
rit.
night! O won-drous night! O night di -
70
a tempo
ff
rit.
vine!

GESU BAMBINO

for S.A.T.B. voices, accompanied

Words by
FREDRICK H. MARTENS (1874-1932)

Music by
PIETRO YON (1886-1943)
Arranged by
MARK HAYES (ASCAP)

Copyright © 2004 by Harold Flammer Music
(A Division of Shawnee Press, Inc.)
International Copyright Secured All Rights Reserved

Duplication of this publication is illegal, and duplication is not granted by the CCLI, LicenSing or OneLicense.net licenses.

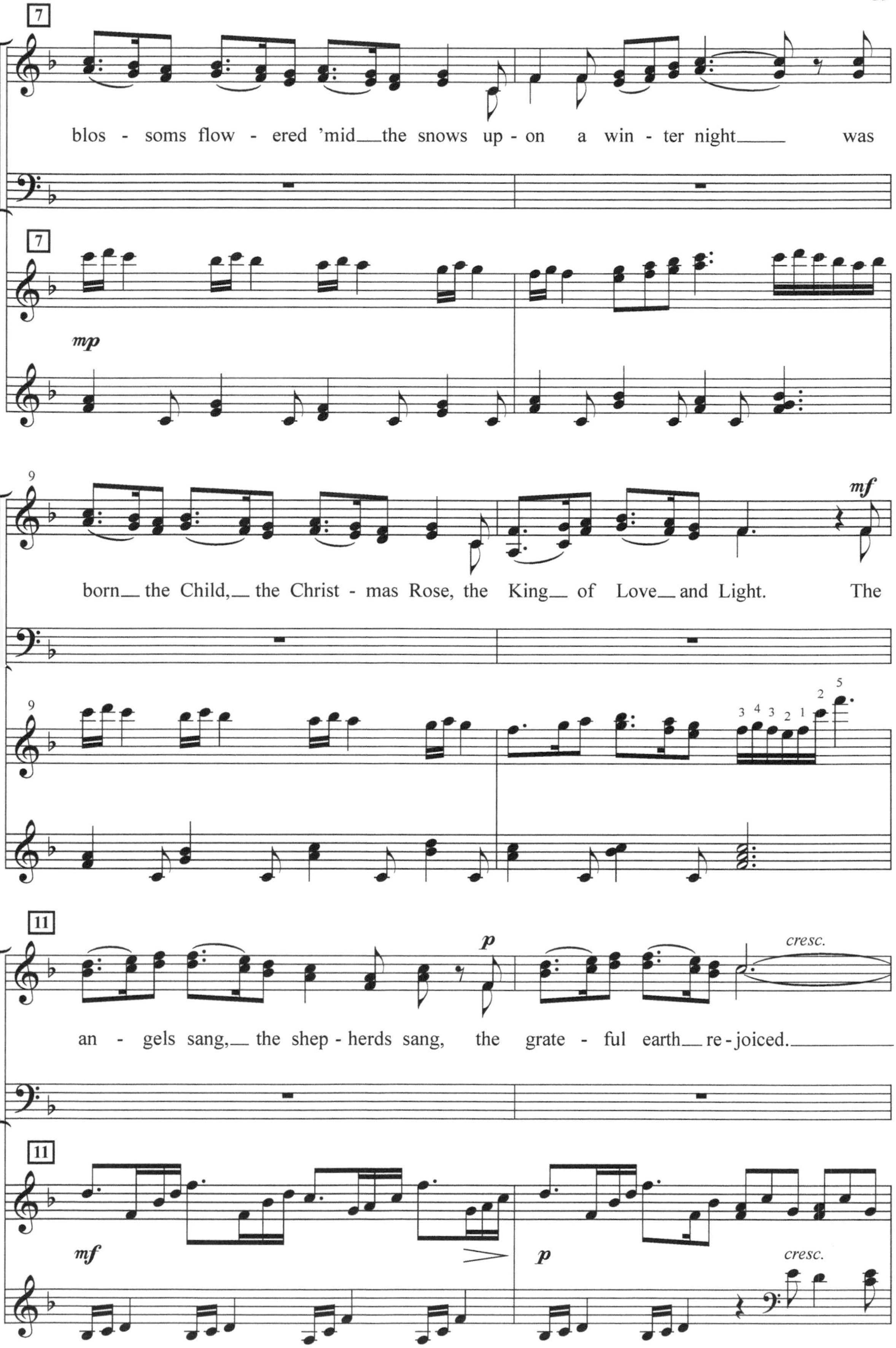
7
blos - soms flow - ered 'mid the snows up - on a win - ter night was
7
mp
9
born the Child, the Christ - mas Rose, the King of Love and Light. The
mf
9
11
p
an - gels sang, the shep - herds sang, the grate - ful earth re - joiced.
cresc.
11
mf
p
cresc.

13
f
And at His bless - ed birth the stars their ex - ul - ta - tion
rit.
sub. pp
16
Slightly faster (♩. = ca. 72)
voiced: "O come, let us a -
17
p
dore Him, O come, let us a -

19
mp
20
dore Him, O come, let us a -
mp
19
20
mp
21
mf
rall.
dore Him, Christ the
mf
21
mf
rall.
23
a tempo
rit.
Lord."
mp
A -
a tempo
23
rit.

25
Andante (♩. = ca. 63)
gain the heart with rap - ture glows to greet the ho - ly night that
mp
27
gave the world its Christ - mas Rose, its King of Love and Light.
mf
Let
29
swell.
ev - 'ry voice ac-claim His name, the grate - ful cho - rus swell, the grate-ful
p
cresc.
mf

31
chorus swell. From par-a-dise to earth He came that we with Him might
dwell.
rit.
34
Slightly faster (♩. = ca. 72)
33
dwell, that we with Him might dwell. O come, let us a-
sub. pp
8vb
35
dore Him, O come, let us a-

37
mp
38
dore
Him,
O
come,
let
us
a
-
mp
37
38
mp
39
mf
rall.
dore
Him,
Christ
the
mf
39
mf
rall.
41
a tempo
rit.
lightly
mf unis.
Lord.
Ah!
mf
O
a tempo
41
mp
rit.

43
a tempo
O come, let us adore Him. Ah!
come, let us a - dore Him, O
43
a tempo
mf
45
A - dore Him, Christ the Lord. O
sub. f
sub. f
come, let us a - dore Him,
45
sub. f
47
p
cresc.
come, O come,
p
cresc.
47
p
cresc.

49

O come, let us a - dore Him.

51

Let us a - dore Him,

pp *cresc.* *f* *rall. e dim.* *mf* *dim.* *sub. p*

Slowly

53

Christ the Lord.

p *rit.* *molto rit.*

DING DONG! MERRILY ON HIGH!

for S.A.T.B. voices, accompanied*

Incorporating
"Ding Dong! Merrily on High"
and "Gentle Mary Laid Her Child"
Arranged by
JOSEPH M. MARTIN (BMI)

* Tune: BRANE DE L'OFFICIAL, from Thoinot Arbeau's *Orchésographie*, 1589
Words: George Ratcliffe Woodward, 1848-1934

Copyright © 2014 by HAL LEONARD - MILWIN MUSIC CORP.
International Copyright Secured All Rights Reserved

Duplication of this publication is illegal, and duplication is not granted by the CCLI, LicenSing or OneLicense.net licenses.

10
sky is riv'n with an - gels sing - ing.
13
S.
A.
Glo - ri - a. Glo -
Glo - ri - a. Glo - ri -
T.
B.
Glo - ri - a.
Glo - ri -
13
16
- ri - a. Glo - ri - a.
a. Glo - ri - a. Ho -
a. Glo - ri - a.
16

19
san - na in ex - cel - sis.
19
mf
25
23
SOPRANO
ALTO
mp unis. (opt. solo)
E'en so here be-low, be - low let
mp
27
stee - ple bells be swung - en; and i - o, i - o, i -

30
o; by priest and peo - ple sung - en.
33
S.
A.
Glo - ri - a. Glo -
Glo - ri - a. Glo - ri -
T.
B.
Glo - ri - a. Glo - ri -
33
36
- ri - a. Glo - ri - a.
a. Glo - ri - a. Ho -
a. Glo - ri - a.
36

* Tune: TEMPUS ADEST FLORIDUM, from *Piae Cantiones*, 1582
Words: Joseph Simpson Cook, 1859-1933

52
man - ger. There He lay, the un - de - filed,
mp
55
57
mf
to the world, a Stran - ger. Son of God of
58
hum - ble birth, beau - ti - ful the sto - ry;

61
praise His name in all the earth. Hail the King of
61
64
Glo - ry.
64
67
mf
67

70
with great celebration
f unis.
Pray ye du - ti - ful - ly prime your mat - in chime, ye
f unis.
70
with great celebration
f
73
ring - ers. May ye beau - ti - ful - ly
73
75
rhyme your eve - time song, ye sing - ers.
75

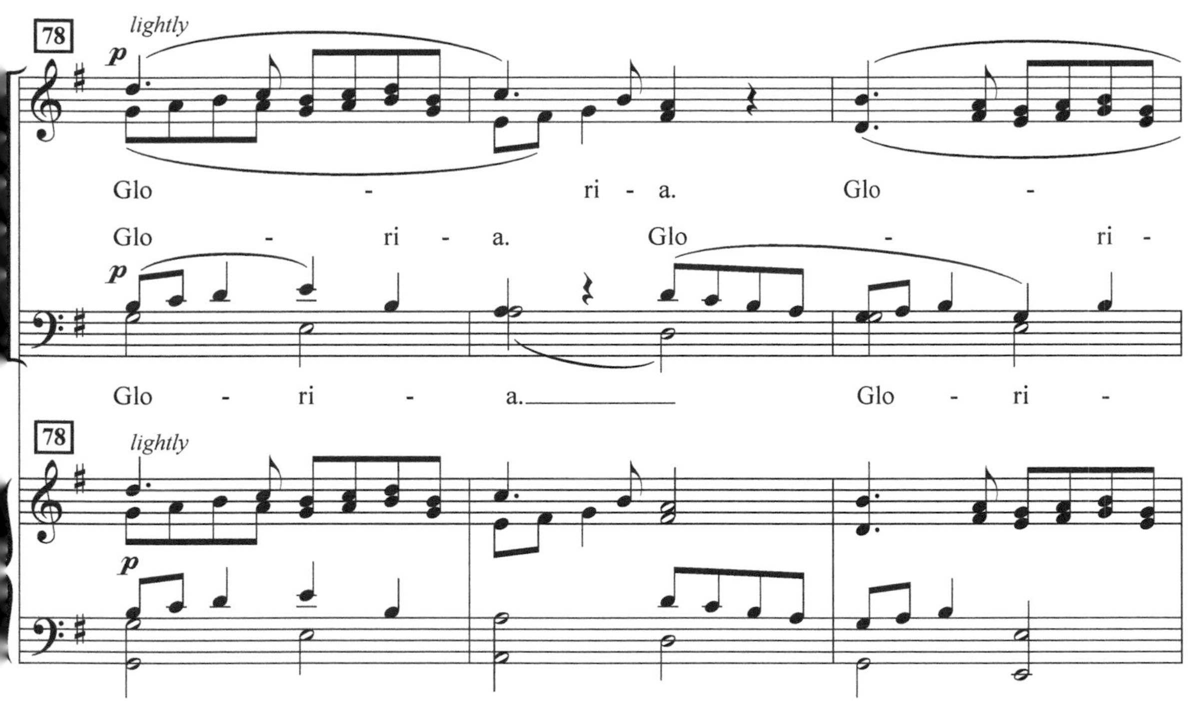
78
lightly
Glo - ri - a. Glo -
Glo - ri - a. Glo - ri -
Glo - ri - a.
Glo - ri -
78
lightly

81
- ri - a. Glo - ri - a.
Ho -
a. Glo - ri - a.
a.
Glo - ri - a.
81

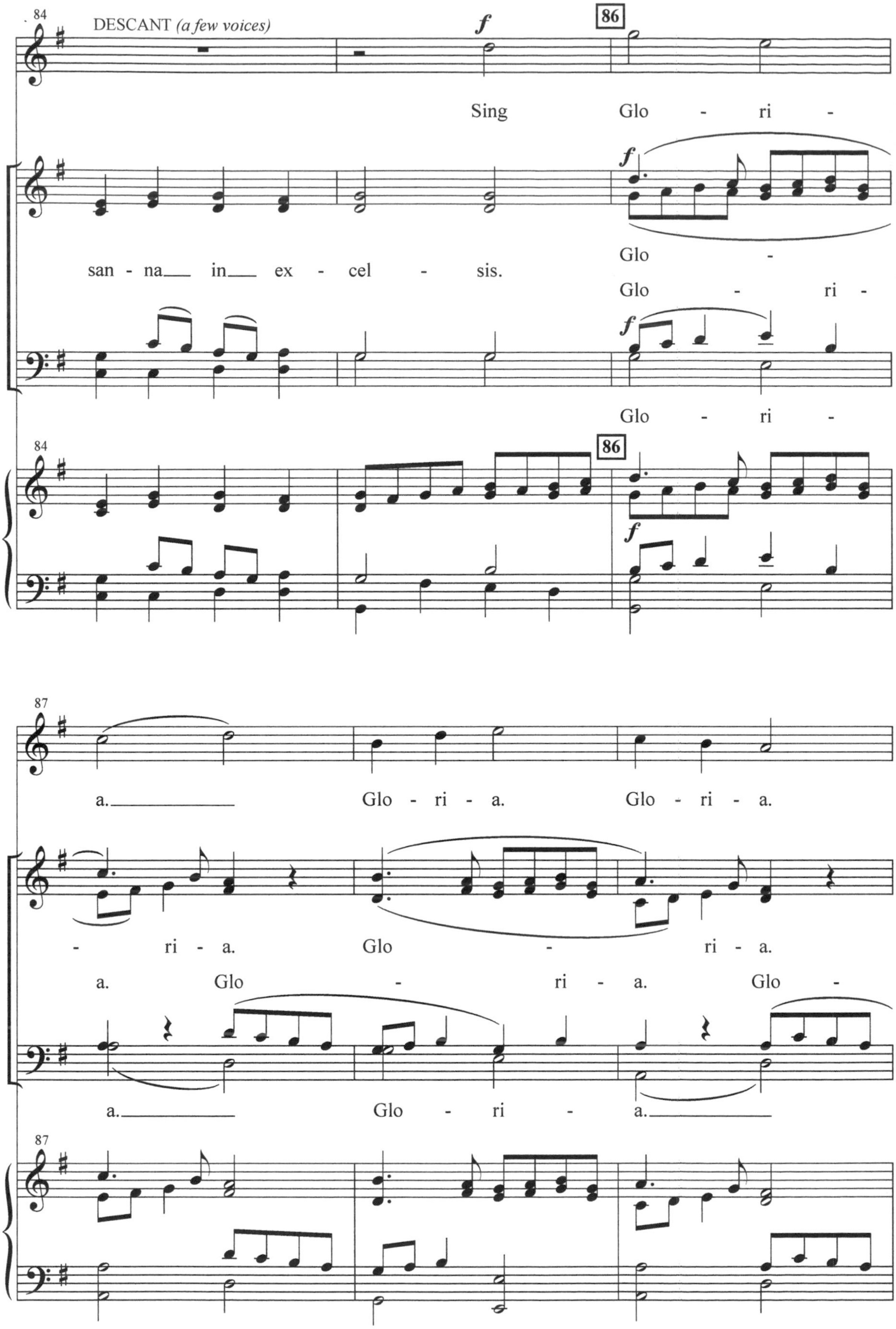
84
DESCANT (a few voices)
f
86
Sing Glo - ri -
san - na in ex - cel - sis.
Glo -
Glo - ri -
Glo - ri -
84
86
87
a.
Glo - ri - a.
Glo - ri - a.
- ri - a.
Glo - ri - a.
a. Glo - ri - a. Glo -
a.
Glo - ri - a.
87

90
92
cresc.
Glo - ri - a. Ho - san - na
Glo - ri - a.
Ho - san - na
- ri - a.
Glo - ri - a.
93
ff
in ex - cel - sis.
in ex - cel - sis.

AS WITH GLADNESS, MEN OF OLD

for S.A.T.B. voices, accompanied

Words by
WILLIAM C. DIX (1837-1898)

Tune: **DIX**
by CONRAD KOCHER (1786-1872)
Arranged by
PEPPER CHOPLIN (ASCAP)

Copyright © 2014 by HAL LEONARD CORPORATION
International Copyright Secured. All Rights Reserved.

Duplication of this publication is illegal, and duplication is not granted by the CCLI, LicenSing or OneLicense.net licenses.

7
as with joy they hailed its light,
9
lead - ing on - ward, beam - ing bright;
11
mp
mf
poco rit.
so, most gra - cious Lord, may we
T.B.
mp
mf
11
mf
poco rit.

a tempo
13
rit.
ev - er - more be led to
15
a tempo
Thee.
cresc.
17
mf unis.
With joy - ful steps they
As with joy - ful steps they sped
mf

19
sped, the man - ger bed,
to that low - ly man - ger bed,
19
21
f
there to bend the knee be - fore
f
21
f
23
mf
mp
Him whom Heav'n and earth a - dore;
mf
mp
23
mf
mp

25
poco rit.
a tempo
mf
so may we with will - ing feet ev - er seek Thy
mer - cy seat. As they of - fered gifts most
rare at the man - ger rough and bare; so may
28
30
31

34
mp
we our trea - sures bring to Christ our heav'n - ly
we our trea - sures bring
34
mp
37
cresc.
unis.
mf
King. Our gifts we of - fer.
mp unis.
mf
O Lord, our gifts we of - fer.
37
3
3
mf
39
f
Ho - ly Je - sus, ev - 'ry day,
f
39
f simile

41
help_ us fol - low in Your_ way.
43
When our_ earth - ly days are past,
45
mf
cresc.
bring our ran - somed souls_ at_ last to

47
f
heav - en's glo - ry, free and bright.
f
47
3 3 3 3 3
f
simile
49
unis.
We shall see Thy ho - ly light.
unis.
49
51
Thou our Light, our Joy, our Crown,
51

53
unis.
Thou our Sun which ne'er goes down;
unis.
53
55
ff
there, for - ev - er may we sing
ff
55
ff
57
ff
al - le - lu - ias to our King!
ff
57
ff

SILENT NIGHT, HOLY NIGHT

for S.A.T.B. voices, accompanied*

Words by
JOSEPH MOHR (1792-1848)

Tune: **STILLE NACHT**
by FRANZ GRUBER (1787-1863)
Arranged by
JOSEPH M. MARTIN (BMI)

* The first two measures may be played by a B♭ Handbell and may be repeated as desired.

Copyright © 2010 by HAL LEONARD - MILWIN MUSIC CORP.
International Copyright Secured. All Rights Reserved.

Duplication of this publication is illegal, and duplication is not granted by the CCLI, LicenSing or OneLicense.net licenses.

10
round yon vir - gin moth - er and Child! Ho - ly In - fant so
10
13
ten - der and mild, sleep in heav - en - ly peace.
13
16
Sleep in heav - en - ly peace.
16
R.H. over

19
mp unis.
Si - lent night,
mp unis.
Si - lent
19
22
ho - ly night, shep - herds quake at the sight.
night, ho - ly night, shep-herds quake at the sight.
22
5
25
Glo - ry streams from hea - ven a - far.
25

27
Heav'n - ly hosts sing "Al - le - lu - ia,
11
29
mf
Christ the Sav - ior is born.
Christ the Sav - ior is
32
mp
born."
34
warmly
Si - lent night,
(Accompanist may double voices if desired.)

35
ho - ly night, Son of God, love's pure light
38
ra - diant beams from Thy ho - ly face, with the dawn of re -
41
mf
rit.
deem - ing grace, Je - sus, Lord, at Thy birth,
mf
44
a tempo
mp
rit.
45
a tempo
Je - sus, Lord, at Thy birth.
mp
44
a tempo
45
a tempo
rit.
mp

SOPRANO DESCANT *(a few voices)*

47

mp

Si - lent night, ho - ly night, star,

CONGREGATION may sing melody

mp

Si - lent night, ho - ly night, won - drous star,

mp

47

50

lend thy light. With the an - gels let us sing

lend thy light. With the an - gels let us sing

50

53
al - le - lu - ia to our King. Christ the Sav - ior is
al - le - lu - ia to our King. Christ the Sav - ior is
53
56
(end descant)
born, Christ the Sav - ior is born.
(end congregation)
born, Christ the Sav - ior is born.
56

59
61
Christ the Sav - ior is born.
unis.
Si - lent night,
62
rit.
Ho - ly, Christ the Sav - ior is
ho - ly night,
65
rit. poco a poco al fine
born.
unis.